Seasons

A Guide To Provide Encouragement In Each Season Of Life.

By Alvastine Bethel

Book Cover Design By: TamikaINK.com

Interior Book Design & Formatting:
TamikaINK.com

Published By: Tamika INK

Library of Congress Cataloging – in- Publication
Data has been applied for.

ISBN: 9798369723173
PRINTED IN THE UNITED STATES OF
AMERICA.

Dedication

This book is dedicated to my loving husband Collin Bethel, my children Tyrik, Collin jr., Tamia, Matthew, Mariah, Cailyn, Courtney; my loving mother Martha Jones, siblings Bobbie (Ariel), Christina (Kendall), Emmanuel (Stephanie), Brittaney and Brion. May God's purpose find each and every one of you and that you find direction, peace, understanding and strength through the words of this book.

I love you all.

Table of Contents

Introduction

Don't be persuaded by what you see. Just as the sun gives way to the moon, seasons will change! Don't give up when it seems as if life is not going according to your plan.

Remember that God's plan for your life supersedes it all! Keep a positive attitude even in the most difficult times of life. Know that there is a reason behind everything. When you understand that God's timing is perfect, you'll began to understand and recognize which season you're in. You will learn how to apply God's word as encouragement and hope to get through the most darkest seasons of life. You will even learn the importance of remaining humble in your high seasons. This will challenge you to become the best version of who God has created and chosen you to be. Understanding, experience, and application comes with time. Continue to ask God for wisdom and knowledge to help keep you in each season of your life!

Seasons

There are four seasons...
Winter, Summer, Spring & Fall. We know the season we are in by what we see or by what we feel. Every year the temperature and weather pattern for each season repeats itself.

In the **fall**; Temperature gradually decreases, and leaves turn in color and start to fall from the trees.

Winter is usually the coldest time of year. Some places brings freezing temperatures and snow.

In the **spring**, plants that were once dormant, begin to grow again, new seedlings sprout out of the ground, and hibernating animals begin to surface the lands.

In the **summer**, the weather grows warmer, and in some areas, the heat translates to drier temperatures. This hot, dry time of year can lead to droughts, where water is in short supply.

It's the same for the spiritual seasons we encounter in our own personal lives.

There are numerous spiritual seasons you will experience over and over in the course of your lifetime. How you view each season and prepare for each season will determine how you make it through.

Ecclesiastes 3

To every thing there is a season, and a time to every purpose under the heaven:
A time to be born, and a time to die; a time to plant, and a time to pluck up that which is planted;
A time to kill, and a time to heal; a time to break down, and a time to build up;
A time to weep, and a time to laugh; a time to mourn, and a time to dance;
A time to cast away stones, and a time to gather stones together; a time to embrace, and a time to refrain from embracing;
A time to get, and a time to lose; a time to keep, and a time to cast away;
A time to rend, and a time to sew; a time to keep silence, and a time to speak;
A time to love, and a time to hate; a time of war, and a time of peace. Kjv

When you began to understand the importance of timing, you'll began to embrace each season with a new perspective!

Planting Season

1 Corinthians 3:6 kjv

I have planted, Apollos watered; but God gave the increase.

When a person plants a seed in the natural, they are expecting a harvest of whatever the type of seed it is that has been planted. So if you plant watermelon seeds, you are expecting a harvest of watermelons to grow in the near future. You have to put in work by using your physical strength to dig a hole in the dirt and place the seeds into the hole.

You know that if you invest your time and care for the seeds, that it will produce the desired results of producing watermelons! Well that's how God is! He uses his people to plant seeds in the lives of others! Seeds can be knowledge, instructions, encouragement, inspiration, God's Word, wisdom and understanding! But the seed being planted, has you waiting with expectation to producing a desired result! We plant, but God produces his desired result in the lives of HIS people!

Sometimes it's our job to plant a seed of an encouraging word into our neighbor. It maybe at a time when they need it most! They may have contemplated suicide earlier that day, but because you told them about the goodness of the Lord, and reminded them of how much God loved them, it changed their mind! While some people tore me down with judgements & Words, because of personal choices I made in life; my life changed because of the people God had around me, that planted seeds of hope into my life. Especially during the years I was lost in sin. Those years where darkness overtook every aspect of my life! And I was to blame. Nobody but me!

There will be seasons of your life where it seems as if you are working alone. You maybe occupied imparting Knowledge into one individual and on another note, you are encouraging someone else. This will be a selfless season. All that you have faced in life up until this point will be used as wisdom to help others change their perspective of where they are! We GO through to help others GROW through!

Keep planting in the lives of others, your season of rest will come. Just be patient and continue to be led by the spirit.

Season of Rest

Matthew 11:28 kjv

Come unto me, all ye that labour and are heavy laden, and I will give you rest.

When you work hard, you will eventually get tired. When you work non-stop, there will come a season of your life where your body will require rest! A person that doesn't know the importance of rest will eventually self-destruct! It's ok to rest your mind, heart and hands. Not just resting your physical body, but God wants to give us the type of rest that we can't obtain anywhere else in this world! We have to meet him where he is. In his presence, there is fullness of joy. There is peace that surpasses all understanding!

The weight of this world can be so heavy at times. Our hearts can be loaded with the cares of this life. So we must learn to come to God through prayer. We must master being in a still position, long enough to hear his instructions. We must also learn to allow God to move in those seasons where he wants us to remain motionless! We mess up when we burn ourselves out trying to accomplish things that God hasn't even told us to do! Rest!!!

Due Season

And let us not be weary in well doing: for in due season we shall reap, if we faint not.
Galatians 6:9 kjv

This is a season where, everything you have sown is getting ready to sprout forward. The crops are ready to be plucked. You are ready to receive everything that you've worked hard for. Sometimes it takes years to receive a harvest of mango trees. But the guarantee of it all, is that after a mango seed has been planted, it will produce! Even in a spiritual aspect! If we sow love, we shall reap love. If we sow years of sacrificing our first fruits to God, we will reap God's best! That's why you must be careful what you are sowing. I know that it gets hard sometimes. I know that you may want to throw in the towel.

Sometimes people may never appreciate you while your toiling, but don't faint. Your reaping season is vastly approaching. Get ready to receive your harvest!

Seasons of Hope

Now faith is the substance of things hoped for, the evidence of things not seen.
Hebrews 11:1 KJV

Everything you have is because of God. There maybe times where you can't see the potential or the outcome, but know that God has more for your life than what you accept or see at the moment. Just don't loose HoPe. Even when life gets hard.

Remember....Things won't be the same always! Seasons change!

Waiting Season

But they that wait upon the LORD shall renew their strength; they shall mount up with wings as eagles; they shall run, and not be weary; and they shall walk, and not faint. Isaiah 40:31 kjv

Wait on the Lord: be of good courage, and he shall strengthen thine heart: wait, I say, on the Lord.
Psalms 27:14 kjv

Waiting is just a major part of life. We wait in the grocery lines at the supermarkets. We wait in concert lines to see our favorite artists. We wait in long lines at our favorite fast food chains for food. We wait in long lines at the airports. We wait at Doctor appointments in the waiting rooms, but when it comes to certain things we pray for, or Spiritual mountains that we need God to move; we want to rush God. I've come to realize that the problem is never in waiting. "The problem shifts to your attitude while you're in your "waiting season." You must learn how to get out of that mentality of wanting everything fast! When you live life that way, you tend to make a lot of mistakes.

You tend to rush things that take time. Time reveals all, but if you're always in a rush, you can miss out on your biggest blessings. During your waiting season, you may feel so many different emotions. You may get tired. You may feel lonely, depressed, frustrated, sad, angry and grow impatient; but God is going to give you strength for the journey. He is going to strengthen your heart! Sometimes God makes us wait for the things we constantly pray for. Sometimes it's because God already knows that we're not ready to accept it. God knows that if it ever ended up in our hands before his time, that we would mess it up. So while you're in your waiting season, look at it as a time for preparation and reflection. Rejoice in advance that God is already working things out for your good. Seasons change. You won't be waiting forever....

Seasons Of Sacrifice

And not only so, but we glory in tribulations also: knowing that tribulation worketh patience; And patience, experience; and experience, hope: Romans 5: 3-4 kjv

According to the New Oxford American Dictionary, the word sacrifice means,"An act of giving up something valued for the sake of something else regarded as more important or worthy." This further lets me know that you will have to sacrifice your personal feelings sometimes. You may have to give up the right for the wrong. You may have to bite your tongue and understand timing. Somethings can't be said all at once. There will be times where it will seem as if you are putting more effort out than others. You will have to learn to keep your eyes on God! You will have a lot of sleepless nights in this season. This will be a time where you will have to pray for wisdom, clarity, understanding and application. Don't give up, because God will go before you in every situation that you will have to face. You have to maintain your joy in this season. The joy of the

Lord will be your strength! God wants us to develop a spirit of patience. Sacrifice in this season now in order to appreciate the blessings to come.

Dry Season

For God is not unrighteous to forget your work and labour of love, which ye have shewed toward his name, in that ye have ministered to the saints, and do minister.
Hebrews 6:10 kjv

There will be times where it seems as if you have been working hard but nothing is producing. You will feel as if God has forgotten all about you. This will be a season where people may leave you alone, but the reassurance that you have is that God will never leave you, nor forsake you. This will be a great time to remove things that maybe hindering your spiritual growth. Examine your heart. The reality is that, we all will go through a season of drought and difficulties. We must continue to trust God in the drought and realize that seasons do change. It won't be this way always!

Pressing Season

Brethren, I count not myself to have apprehended: but this one thing I do, forgetting those things which are behind, and reaching forth unto those things which are before, 14. I press toward the mark for the prize of the high calling of God in Christ Jesus.
Philippians 3:13-14 kjv

Have you ever been in a season where it seems as if you have to put extra energy into accomplishing things? A season where you maybe tired mentally or physically, and you maybe on the brink of giving up? I want to encourage you to hold on my sister and brother. Remember seasons change. Everything we do in this life must be done with the prize in mind. The higher calling which is in Christ Jesus. This will be a season where you have to leave some memories, people, places, and things behind in order to advance. God has better in store for you up the road. Your next level is in arms reach.

Remember we belong to God. He created us with purpose, so keep pressing. Press through the shame. Press through disappointment. Press through loneliness. Press through fear and doubt.

Seasons Of Change

Therefore if any man be in Christ, he is a new creature. Old things are passed away; behold all things become new.
2 Corinthians 5:17 kjv

It's impossible for things to stay the same in our lives once we've had an encounter with God. You must understand that life is guaranteed to change. Change is something that we often fear, when in reality change maybe a blessing in disguise. The attitude we carry,
paired with our perspective concerning the changes in our lives, will dictate how we overcome. You maybe hesitant to make adjustments, because you are comfortable where you are. God wants to give you a new life, and if you say you are God's child; then your life must indicate a change. From the way you walk, talk and live; let the word of God do the work. Don't fight change, embrace it. Sometimes we try to hold onto people and situations that God wants us to release. We are reluctant to trust God, because of what's familiar. You must

understand that you will prolong the greater blessings that God has in store for you. Real change can't occur unless you allow God to have full control over your life.

Seasons Of Conviction

And they which heard it, being convicted by their own conscience, went out one by one, beginning at the eldest, even unto the last: and Jesus was left alone, and the woman standing in the midst.
John 8:9 kjv

It's a good thing to be in a place where you feel convicted when you say or do something you know is not right. It keeps you humbled. We all are human and we all need God's grace. His grace is sufficient. No worries. Dry your eyes and pick yourself back up. No need to stay stuck in guilt when you fall short of God's word. Convicted but not cast down. Recover and press forward!

Seasons Of Instructions

He that hath ears to hear, let him hear.
Matthew 11:15 kjv

You will be in a season where God will deal with you on a personal level of what he wants to do in your life. This is the time you need to get as close to God as possible.

Eliminate all distractions, so that he can reveal where he's trying to take you. It's easy to hear a word from man, but it's an entirely different level when you allow God to really order your steps. God gives instructions sometimes through dreams, his prophets or he will minister through scripture specifically to you. We need instructions to bake cakes and to prepare our favorite delicious dishes. Why can't we trust God completely with the instructions he wants to give us for our lives? Prepare your heart and mind to receive your instructions for the next level he's taking you to.

Speaking Season

Death and life are in the power of the tongue: and they that love it shall eat the fruit thereof.
Proverbs 18:21 kjv

This will be a season where you will either choose to live abundantly by what you speak or die spiritually by what you say. Your level of thinking must change. You'll understand that your words have power. You must learn to decree and declare your days. Whatever you dwell on will be. When you understand that your tongue can change the course of your life, you'll speak boldly and carefully.

Seasons Of Strategy

And the Lord answered me, and said, Write the vision, and make it plain upon tables, that he may run that readeth it.
For the vision is yet for an appointed time, but at the end it shall speak, and not lie: though it tarry, wait for it; because it will surely come, it will not tarry.
Habakkuk 2 kjv

In this season, this will be a time for you to strategize. Whatever you want God to do in your life, write it down. Make it plain. Then write how you will execute it. This will be a season of your life where you may need to seek professional and spiritual guidance, in order to effectively strategize your plans. With prayer and a plan, you will go far. Stay in the Will of God. Keep your mouth closed, your eyes open and run!

Seasons Of Doubt

But let him ask in faith, nothing wavering. For he that wavereth is like a wave of the sea driven with the wind and tossed.
James 1:6 kjv

This will be a season where you will have to stand firm on God's word. Not doubting in thought, deeds or words. Everything you see, speak & do, must be done through faith. There will be no time for second guessing. If you ask God for something and you believe in your heart that it will happen; this is not the time to doubt. If God sends his prophet with a word concerning your life, don't doubt it. Everything will happen in God's timing.

Move according to the spirit of God. Don't allow circumstances, people or things to cause you to doubt. Change your thought process. Have faith that it will happen to you and for you! Eliminate all doubt!

Seasons Of Restoration

And I will restore to you the years that the locust hath eaten, the cankerworm, and the caterpillar, and the Palmer worm, my great army which I sent among you.
Joel 2:25 kjv

Sometimes you will take substantial losses. Life and the things of this world will drain your soul. You may have just experienced taking losses to your finances, family and friends, that can ultimately weaken your faith. Don't loose hope. Don't get frustrated, God will restore everything the enemy thought he took away from you. Pause. Take a deep breath. God is going to restore your mind back. He's going to restore your peace.

He's going to restore your family. He's going to restore your finances. He's even capable of restoring your health. Is there anything too hard for God? Restoration season is here!

Seasons Of Focus

Let thine eyes look right on, and let thine eyelids look straight before thee
Proverbs 4:25 kjv

Stay focused in this season. You won't have time to be sidetracked. You don't have time to be discouraged by attacks sent intentionally to knock you off your feet. Adjust your eyesight on where God is taking you. Stay the course and put your mind and heart in God's hands. He will work things out in this season for you. No need to worry. He's in control of it all. Keep your focus off people and adjust your eyesight on God. You can really miss what God is trying to do for you in this season, if you don't keep your eyes on him. Our sight has to go beyond what we see in the moment. Don't be persuaded by what you see and allow it to make you miss your blessing in this season.

Seasons Of Preparation

Prepare thy work without, and make it fit for thyself in the field; and afterwards build thine house.
Proverbs 24:27 kjv

This will be a season where you will put things in order. Prepare your mind, heart, soul and life, in order to receive what God is about to bless you with. You will prioritize things and reclaim your time. No more waisted time. It's time to walk upright and invest in yourself. Confidence will be your best friend. There will be no more time for doubt. There will be no more missed opportunities. Put your best foot forward. If you need training in certain areas, invest! Cover all weak points in your life. Pray for strength and resources in this season. Prepare for what God has already promised you!

Seasons of Joy

Then he said unto them, Go your way, eat the fat, and drink the sweet, and send portions unto them for whom nothing is prepared: for this day is holy unto our Lord: neither be ye sorry; for the joy of the Lord is your strength. Nehemiah 8:10 kjv

In this season, the joy of the Lord will be your strength to make it through life's trials. Not the joy we receive from how people, places or the things that we possess makes us feel. It will be through our relationship with God that will propel us to the next season. This will be a season of unspeakable joy. People won't be able to comprehend the smile on your face. Even with chaos all around, God will give you joy! Continue to smile in the good times, as well as the bad times. Remember that this type of joy can't be given, nor taken away by this world.

Seasons Of Peace

These things I have spoken unto you, that in me ye might have peace. In the world ye shall have tribulation: but be of good cheer; I have overcome the world.
John 16:33 kjv

This will be a season where you must realize that there is no peace apart from God. After you've searched high and low. After you've tried everything and everything has failed, you will learn to try Jesus. People, places and things can only give temporary fulfillment. Remember, there is no peace apart from God. He will give you the peace that surpasses all understanding. When there is darkness in your life, and you are in the middle of a storm, you will still have peace knowing that God will take care of you. Always know that God is in control, and that he is concerned about the things that concerns you. So rest your weary heart and mind. Seek the Lord while he may be found. Watch the
inexplainable peace you feel when you find him.

Seasons Of Suffering

If we suffer, we shall also reign with him: if we deny him, he also will deny us.
2 Timothy 2:12 kjv

My Apostle Dr. Barbara Broussard once said that "suffering is good for you". I couldn't understand what she meant until I began to mature in God. I've come to realize that suffering produces patience. Suffering brings out strengths in you that you'd never knew you had. Suffering is a part of life. If we say we are God's children, we must learn how to suffer. Once we realize we can't change certain situations in our lives, but that we do
have control on how we view certain situations; is when we will win! Jesus even suffered, but he said, "Nevertheless not my will, but thine, be done." We must understand that our assignment has to supersede what we may feel at the present moment. It's greater than us sometimes. Stop looking at the situations and

seek to understand your assignment. Remember we suffer to one day Reign!

Seasons of Separation

Who shall separate us from the love of Christ? shall tribulation, or distress, or persecution, or famine, or nakedness, or peril, or sword?
As it is written, For thy sake we are killed all the day long; we are accounted as sheep for the slaughter.
Nay, in all these things we are more than conquerors through him that loved us.
For I am persuaded, that neither death, nor life, nor angels, nor principalities, nor powers, nor things present, nor things to come,
Nor height, nor depth, nor any other creature, shall be able to separate us from the love of God, which is in Christ Jesus our Lord. Romans 8:35-39 kjv

In this season we will have to learn how to separate from anyone or anything that tries to separate us from the love of God! There is nothing in this world that should come before your relationship with Christ! You must understand how much God loves you.

You must understand that God only wants the best for you. God's love will find you wherever you are. Remember that God promised to always be there for us. We are the ones that tend to let wedges and space form between our bond with God. Not in this season. Separate from everything that tries to deter you from fulfilling your purpose in God!

Seasons Of Growth

But grow in grace, and in the knowledge of our Lord and Saviour Jesus Christ. To him be glory both now and forever.
2 Peter 3:18 kjv

This will be a time where you put everything you've ever experienced to use. There is no greater feeling like growing in God. Grow through reading the word of God, and applying it to your lives. Understanding that you're here because of God's grace and nothing good that you could've done. Growth is such a beautiful thing. Embrace it!

Seasons Of Forgiveness

If we confess our sins, he is faithful and just to forgive us our sins and to cleanse us from all unrighteousness.
1 John 1:9 kjv

This is a very hard season. Forgiveness sounds easy to do, but when you experience hurt on a level that you'd never thought possible; it can make this process very difficult. How do you forgive someone who tries to destroy your character? How do you forgive someone that has harmed you? How do you forgive someone who has tried to destroy your life? You must first admit how things have affected you. Then you must make a choice to forgive them. Forgiveness doesn't happen over night. It's a constant process. Some days you'll have doubts, but if we understand that ultimately, we all are in need of grace; then and only then will our healing take place. This season may not even be about forgiving others. You may have to forgive yourself, and know that you are worthy. We all have a past and some of our pasts aren't very pretty. You must realize that God can still use you for his glory. You are special and you can't go far with things bottled up inside of your heart. Feelings of inadequacy and unworthiness. Not loving yourself, nor believing in yourself, are some of the tactics the enemy uses to keep you bound.

Forgive yourself and others. Watch the load lift from your heart!

Seasons Of Healing

He healeth the broken in heart, and bindeth up their wounds.
Psalm 147:3 kjv

This will be a season where healing will take place. In your mind, as well as your body and soul. God wants you whole. That means your mind intact, as well as your body. A lot of times we use concealment as a ploy. We look great on the outside, but we are broken into a million pieces on the inside. You will cry your last tear in this season. Be ready for your healing to begin. Hurt people, hurt people. You don't ever want to be in a position where you bleed on the ones sent by God to save you! Take your time and heal properly.

Heal from past traumas. Heal from words. Heal from abandonment issues. Heal from what others may have done. Heal from the inside out. Let God complete the work. Get ready to introduce the best version of yourself! Your next level depends on you healing!

Seasons Of Accountability

What shall we say then? Shall we continue in sin, that grace may abound?
Romans 6:1 kjv

Taking accountability is critical in this season. Accountability is taking ownership of what you say and do. Blaming others for where you presently are, will be no more. You will mature in this season. You will understand that you can create the life you desire.

You will realize that every choice comes with consequences. Therefore, you will learn to choose wisely. You must give an answer for the areas you are working on in your life.

What can I do to improve this? Why did I do this? Ask God to help you in the areas you may struggle in. Pray for discipline.

Selfless Season

I protest by your rejoicing which I have in Christ Jesus Our Lord, I die daily.
1 Corinthians 15:31 kjv

This will be a season where you have to give more than you receive. You will give more of yourself to kingdom work. You will have to sacrifice how you feel the majority of the time, and seek to understand others more than fighting to be heard. You will have to die to your feelings and your way of doing things; daily. You will give your time, talent and treasures in this season. As you feel depleted, you must be surrounded by those who can pour back into your spirit man. You'll feel mentally drained most times. This season won't last always, but it's necessary in becoming who God has destined you to be.

Me Season

Wherefore, my beloved, as ye have always obeyed, not as in my presence only, but now much more in my absence, work out your own salvation with fear and trembling.
Philippians 2:12 kjv

This will be a season where you must put "you" first. If you are no good to yourself, how can you be any good to anyone else? You will have to learn how to think for yourself, pray for yourself, and make decisions for yourself. You will have to go to God for yourself. Developing a personal relationship with God where you can hear from him for yourself. This will also be a time for you to make critical moves in your personal life. What are some things you've always wanted to do? What are some places you've always wanted to go? Put your feelings and needs above anything else. Clear the clutter in your space. Encourage yourself. This will be a time of Self-Evaluation. Use the Bible as a mirror to see yourself in scripture. Ask God to transform and renew your mind.

When you start putting your needs and wants above anything or anyone else; don't be surprised who no longer walks beside you in this season. Take breaks as you need them. It's ok to pick a day to lay in bed and decide to do nothing. Relax your mind. Visit your favorite restaurant. Set boundaries in your life. Establish order in your house. Dance like you've never danced before. Don't be so hard on yourself. Learn balance! Work hard, but play harder.

Fighting Season

For we wrestle not against flesh and blood, but against principalities, against powers, against the rulers of the darkness of this world, against spiritual wickedness in high places. Ephesians 6:12 kjv

This will be a season where you will have to fight in the spiritual realm. Through prayer, fasting and speaking God's word over situations of life. You will be in a spiritual battle. You will have to be on high alert at all times. You will have to plead the blood over your home, your spouse, your children, your church, your job and your community. Don't get distracted. Know that the enemy often uses those that are close to us. So be keen to satan's tactics. Arm yourselves with the word of God.

13 *Wherefore take unto you the whole armour of God, that ye may be able to withstand in the evil day, and having done all, to stand.* ***14*** *Stand therefore, having your loins girt about with truth, and having on the breastplate of righteousness;****15*** *And your feet shod with the* *preparation of the gospel of peace;* **16** *Above all, taking the shield of faith, wherewith ye shall be able to quench all the fiery darts of the wicked.* **17** *And take the helmet of salvation, and the sword of the Spirit, which is the word of God: Ephesians 6:13-17 kjv*

Just know that the victory is already won. Go through the motions. Whatever you do, don't give up! Keep fighting!

Lonely Season

For our light affliction, which is but for a moment, worketh for us a far more exceeding and eternal weight of glory.
2 Corinthians 4:17 kjv

Loneliness is an internal feeling. Loneliness might be something you may experience in this season, or loneliness might be necessary in this season to prepare you for what's to come. You have to learn how to be alone. How to have your own identity. Life will show you that you will only be able to depend on God. You will learn how to be ok in this season. Everyone won't be apart of your growth in this season. You will only be able to operate off the words and strength of God! A Season where it seems as if you have no one to call! Don't worry, because God is up to something. He's about to send the right help at the right time! This journey may get lonely, but Jesus promises to be with us always!

Seasons of A Great Fall

For a just man falleth seven times, and riseth up again.
Proverbs 24:16 kjv

Everyone will experience this season. This season tests and builds character. We all go through moments of pride. Moments where we feel as if we've arrived. Life will show you how to remain humble, because pride comes before a great fall. This will be a season where you will have to do some self-evaluation. What are some things that I need to change about myself? You will have to ask God for forgiveness and humble yourself before God.

Sometimes positions, titles, status, materialistic things, friends, family and opportunities will make you feel as if you're untouchable. They will make you feel as if you've obtained them by your own strength. You must realize that we can't do nothing without God. It's in him that we live, breathe, move and have our being. Prepare for the fall, but you will rise again after this season. You will be better than before, but you'll realize with God on your side, you can't fail!

Seasons Of Establishment

Ponder the path of thy feet, and let all thy ways be established.
Proverbs 4:26 kjv

You must carefully consider where you are going in this season. Make sure you are walking in the right direction, as well as on the right path. When you ponder before you make a move, your paths will be established. This means wherever you go, will be secured. Carefully consider God's word concerning your life. When you understand that you were created for so much more, you'll understand that you must walk carefully.

Seasons Of Grace

And he said unto me, My grace is sufficient for thee: for my strength is made perfect in weakness. Most gladly therefore will I rather glory in my infirmities, that the power of Christ may rest upon me.
2 Corinthians 12:9 kjv

Extend grace not only to others, but yourself. Allow yourself to make mistakes. You grow from mistakes. Always look for the lessons in trials, but learn how to quickly get back up again. When people don't show you grace, just know that God's grace is sufficient. It's enough! You're loved by God more than you'll ever know.

About Alvastine Bethel

Alvastine Bethel is known for uplifting, motivating, and encouraging others. She has a heart for people and is a powerful example of strength and perseverance for today's young generation. She is a retired Correctional Officer of 18 years. She holds an

Associate Degree in Arts and is currently continuing her education through the Bachelor's program in Criminal Justice at Florida International University. She is a devoted wife and mother to her beautiful family. She is currently one of the youth pastors at Church Of The Rock. She is one of the owners of "The Game Cave" and "Planted with a Purpose." Her podcast entitled "Planted with a Purpose" can be heard on digital platforms such as Spotify and anchor. She is currently the program officer for CORYP. Which is a youth program that is on the horizon and will be committed to ensuring children have opportunities to be cared for and supported in their development, by supportive services in their communities. She is a certified firearms instructor and loves to teach and give words of wisdom to growing youth.

Connect with Alvastine Bethel
Email: alvastinej1984@gmail.com
IG: Planted_With_A_Purpose
FB: Al Bethel
Tik Tok: Planted with a purpose
Twitter: Planted with a purpose

www.ingramcontent.com/pod-product-compliance
Lightning Source LLC
LaVergne TN
LVHW052103160826
845678LV00015B/3331

* 9 7 9 8 3 6 9 7 2 3 1 7 3 *